I0542021

Movements

Movements

SYMPHONIC
POEMS

RIVKA EPSTEIN HATTIN

HEADSTAND
PRESS

Copyright © 2024 Rivka Epstein Hattin

All rights reserved. No part of this publication may be reproduced, distributed, or transmitted in any form by any means, including photocopying, recording, or other electronic methods without the prior written permission of the author, except in the case of brief quotations embodied in reviews and certain other noncommercial uses permitted by copyright law. For permission requests, write to the author at the email address below.

movements.poems@gmail.com

ISBN 978-965-93207-0-7

Published by Headstand Press
Cover design by Lindsay Lusby, Natalie Friedemann-Weinberg,
& Rivka Epstein Hattin
Cover background photo by Meriç Dağlı on Unsplash
Author photo by Leeba Hattin
Book interior by Lindsay Lusby
Typeset in Adobe Caslon Pro, Vatican, and Bree

Printed in the United States of America

First Printing, 2024

Contents

ALLEGRO CON BRIO

ANDANTE CANTABILE

SCHERZO CON MOTO

RONDO ESPRESSIVO

CADENZA

Elegy for Yakir

HY"D

You asked me what I was writing about,
but before I could speak,
your light ascended.

Once partners at the ivory keyboard,
racetrack,
concert hall,
holiday table, house of prayer.

Now we are left.
With words. Without words.

I gift you these poems. Perhaps love can reach that high.

We will meet again
in a better world.

And we will play Beethoven together.

*Yakir Hexter, my dear nephew, was a budding architect,
erudite scholar, and supreme athlete who fought honorably to protect us.
He fell in battle in the Southern Gaza strip on January 8, 2024.
His legacy continues to inspire us.*

Muse of Transcendence

craft me
move me
lift me
take me beyond
what is here
what is now
deliver me
to bliss
to Eden
to tomorrow

Allegro con brio

Crafting Her

Not an empty mayonnaise jar
nor a pathetically overdrawn bank account.
Not a deserted beehive
nor a trampled bubblegum wrapper.

Not the burned-out carcass of a roadside car
nor the viper's shrugged-off argyle skins.
Not the lonely clinking of last night's cocktail tumblers
nor the hollow black bowels of the twisted French horn.

Rather the warm belly of an expectant sheep
and the unbearable fullness of an overblown red balloon.
Rather the brimming mug's edge hugging the cinnamon tea
and the final proud chords of the hour-long symphony.

Rather the smooth-pebbled mouth of the centered village
    well
and the deep denim pocket on faded king-sized overalls.
Rather the chocolate memory that lingers long after the
    quick swallow
and the ringing bells' song that is hanging in the wet
    Prague air.

Crafting her from within, from beyond,
with fibers that hold and tones that rise.
Crafting her to last, but mindful of the balance—
    the material,
        the immaterial.

Autumn's Studio

Autumn has her moods,
like Picasso, ranting in blue,
she stomps her heavy-heeled boot,
worrying garden blooms enough
to take their leave at once
without a farewell note or nod.

Autumn drinks too often
and leaves the leaves
to droop low,
wallowing closer to the ground
than they should.
Her ally
gravity
always wins the tug of war
between what should fly
but instead will wither.

Autumn forces her gutsy way
through the stone cottage door,
ignoring locked storm windows and doubly thatched roofs.

There is no silencing her howling nightsong
or her flapping flaming costume of crimson.
Gusts and gales refuse to be tempered
and her stormy episodes only increase in duration and
   frequency,
deeming her incurable.

Perhaps all one can do is join her
in the splattered artist's studio
as her oily colors and matted brushes
fly madly around her
and her ear-splitting cackles rebound
from every wall.

Perhaps all one can do is sit
beside her as her swirling fits work
their way out,
leaving a cold hollow stillness in their wake
soon filled with ice and blue.

Date with Fred

We're floating on a frozen block with no time signature
    and a broken metronome.
Notes are free-falling, and Chopin is laughing so hard I can
    see down his colon.
His ice-white quill is useless now and his piano is colliding
    overhead with a fiery comet.
"Frederic," I begin, "How did you make a break—
how did you free yourself from what the masters
fed you up as truth for breakfast?"
His blank stare returns with the words,
"I skipped meals and never once ate in the cafeteria."
But Chopin is not really listening to me,
no wasting time with the pestering simpletons.
He is busy watching
the keys cascading down from the upper realms,
combusting as they explode in synchrony.
He is busy noticing
the obvious pattern in chaos—
the rhythm of self-destruction that begets
a new science of counting
without numbers.

He is busy composing a prelude,
demanding fresh ears
that don't wear seatbelts
on the highway.

Puzzling

Piecing the shards back together,
yesterday's confetti glued to my sole,
glued to my soul.
The blisters on my heel
from too much dancing
and from traversing Broadway
one time too many.
The smoky scent stuck to my black T-shirt
despite my desperate attempts to douse my clothes
in perfume.
Desperate.
Piecing the nonsensical parts together,
trying to force two different puzzles
into one framed scene,
knowing the pieces can't, won't bend,
blend,
prongs and crevices frozen,
but played by insistent hands.

Trying to make sense of the game,
prodding unions that repel
like brother and brother,
like icy soil resisting sun,
like too much family
who had no choice.

Feeling Dangerous

I woke up this morning
feeling Dangerous.
I knew it
when the rays hit my
darkened pupils straight-on
like Robin Hood's shot,
piercing my bulging sack.
I was had
and glad of it.
Mounting my muscled steed,
my chest puffed high,
I rode out of my 'hood
and into the day
knowing I would return
different
because Action was beckoning me,
begging
on her squared knees
for my daring.
And I would, I would.

Leaping over fences
that existed only
in my caged adulthood,
I shed the years
like yesterday's wool,
easily felled.
What had taken me so long
to fly?

Noisy Girl

when she was young
she used fourteen rolls of toilet paper
to weave a wedding gown

when she was little
she took notes
carried a clipboard
called a board meeting
time to downsize the company she stated

limelight was her drink of choice
and she pranced her way through hearts
like a bullet train through the village square

the ones on the other side
only heard the swoosh
and told the tale for years after

she grew taller
she grew wiser
she grew plants
that filled her room
with greens and expectations
but couldn't fill her heart

all the words in all the notebooks
can't fill a heart

wearing her purple cowboy boots
that chili pepper babe
hunting for hope
took off

just like that

Quiet Girl

jet-black eyelashes
ivory complexion
blood-red lips that crack
a winning smile
hungry eyes that consume galaxies whole
masterminding stupefying not-once-crying
ever

don't mistake silent
for shallow
don't hug her long

fiddles with a force that
yet again
brings down Jericho's walls

calculating so fast that
the bald professors tear

when the stars perform on their velvet stage above
at the darkest hour of night
her lips move soundless
over the love letters of David the King

picking out the words that
power her calculator and
fill her fiddle's belly
she's feeding on eternity
spitting out the pits

you want in
but the club of one
rarely admits new members
and this ain't your day

the quiet girl
can't hold her tight
the driven goddess
mixing pixels, paint, and gunpowder
like it's a casual drink

uninterested in being noticed
makes her impossible to ignore

BAM!

Eden

creamy cheeks with peach fuzz
open brilliant eyes that refuse to close
curls that wrap around a thousand discoveries a day
and a smile that says
never release me
Eden is not a place
Eden is a star no one can ever reach
because it exists farther than we can measure
it exists to remind us that time will pass
and so will we—
but the stars they stay
they pray
with a last breath that never comes

Snorting Bliss

I want the kind of happiness
that kicks up three feet off the ground
unafraid of landing on bedrock

I want the type of happiness
that whispers to me
in my dark corner
that it's OK to be alone
because the morning sun and evening breeze understand
and promise to be there tomorrow

I want the sort of joy
that sips a piña colada with me and winks
because my jokes are getting better as my
gray hairs multiply

I want the kind of bliss
that kisses me to sleep
and stays all night in my arms
through dreams of me falling off the Earth

I want the sort of laughter
that rises from the deep belly and exits through my nostrils
making my eyes tear and nose run freely
shocking my kids who don't know that
moms can snort

I want a smile wide and sure
that warms others in their dark corners
and convinces the weak
that we can move—even forward—
smiling

Muse of Consolation

when it's gone wrong
spoon-
feed me comfort words
that thaw the frozen heart
unearth a silence that
soothes
better than
sound
grant clear vision
for the blind
spots

Andante cantabile

Beside Me, Angels

discharged from luminous clouds
they join us
in the guise of challenge
in the disguise
of angry neighbors bitching
about dripping garbage bags
in the form of angst
costumed as
inflexible bosses
who don't appreciate out-of-the-box solutions
in the hope of healing
dressed as
proud doctors and numbed patients
angels walk before us
rerouting paths
even dropping
tacks on the trail
whether we're barefooted
or mountain-booted
convinced we can manage it
though we protest
and tantrum
and carry on something awful

because impossible obstacles are not appreciated before
enough sunsets fall
between pain and illumination

When It's Gone Wrong

to the drink
to the keyboard
to the empty yellowed field

to the rooftop
to the noisy sea
to the black-and-white symphony

to the liquor cabinet
to the classics
to the cheek of tender life

to the foamy tub
to the Book of Psalms
to my reflection
worn but true

Yesterday's Leggings

can't stand the smell
of yesterday's leggings
after they warmed me
on the frosty path

can't believe the headlines
in yesterday's paper
after the meltdown
of modernity

can't crack a nut
with a spoon or fork
no matter how hard
I whack it

can't trust a friend
who's shared more
history than heart

can sniff the dawn's
first breath and skip
through the day
believing

can sing
an ancient prayer
unleashing melodies
that matter

can peel back
a flaming orange
and share its
pulpy sweetness

can find a love
that lasts and kiss
with all my mouth

Unearthing Silence

there is a quiet that lives in the middle of our planet
no shovel can reach
no ray can find
a silence that welcomes listeners
humble enough to put ear to earth
and wait
sometimes longer than is comfortable
for the sounds to fade

rumbling traffic
stomping feet
screeching protests
hungry wailing
raging trumpets
crashing markets
angry hissing
deafening explosions
then
an abrupt and eerie stillness
that will not hold

there is a quiet that lives in the middle of our planet
a silence that welcomes listeners
humble enough to put ear to earth
and wait
for what may seem like forever
to hear nothing
but to hear everything

Go Forth, Mouse

Go forth,
gray mouse,
shivering in your dusty hole.

You can seek
your cheese
or your cheesecake
or your cheesy humor.

Why, you can study
astrophysics
and be the first
rodent
to walk on Mars
in a flame-resistant
foil space suit
that effectively
prevents whisker-singeing!

Go forth,
gray mouse,
shivering in your dusty hole.
You can covet
freedom
and renounce
fear
so your trepidatious paws
can march confidently
in a blaring brass parade.
Who says
mice can't play trombone
and stay in perfect step
with the band?

Go forth,
gray mouse.
Dare to dream
that your nightmares
can become your dreams.

Down the Turnpike

Dear Friend or Ex-Friend who needs to be
upcycled or given to the compost pile
so the good parts get used
but the broken parts get trashed
so the thing isn't dangerous with the sharp edges.

Dear Friend or Ex-Friend who needs to do
some healing or grieving or both
so the toxic fumes streaming from
that smooth breath get redirected to a brick chimney that
    can tolerate
carbon emissions
better than my soft heart.

Do you know the sequoia grove down the turnpike
that offers free lectures on Mondays?
Tree lessons
for slow humans.
Like: You must treat the big trees the way we treat the
    elders of our village.
Like: Roots are meant to tangle.
Like: Cut us down at your own risk, for you will go down
harder and first.

Dear Friend or Ex-Friend:
You are welcome
next Monday
down the turnpike.

Global Flop-Up 101

You blew in here
uninvited
and took up residence
in our home
our neighborhood
our temple
our toilet
our truck—
affecting our rhythms
our rhymes
our challenged children
now home eternally going out of their minds.

You crash-landed
in the safest of places,
ripping through every
buffer we thought we'd built.
You know, you deserve a medal—
you do.
For wreaking havoc on a consummate level.
Why, you've earned a freaking Fulbright.

Global Flop-Up 101,
congrats on making the big time.
Every local channel and printed front page,
every concert date, dinner conversation, wedding invite,
    obituary
bears your signature
and stamp of desperation.
Now, can you go back
to where you came from
and leave us our modern psalms
to write?

Blind Spot

I, like the other small people,
believed years ago
that solutions
would fall
like manna
collected,
like clockwork.
As surely as
happily
ever after is printed
on that last page.
It would be
just
apple-pie fine.
But, no,
say the scars
on my once-firm belly,
days don't read like
children's fables.
Hey, heads
get knocked around
on downhill drops
even at the summer fairground.

Learn to be your own sunshine,
and sometimes that means
moving the loaded terracotta pot
from the shaded corner.
And sure!
Drop the fertilizer
like fool's gold—
generously
dazzlingly.
Illumination is not
on the takeout menu.
But—if you are fortunate—
you may catch a ray
from behind
the blind spot.

I Give Up

I give up my sureness that
there are answers.
I give up my pride that
I did it right.
I give up my knowing that
you did your best
because maybe you didn't
and that is just fine.
I give up the illusion that
faith is solid
and that
troubles end
and that
schnapps is for Saturdays.

I give up the trick of juggling endless needs
cuz there's no point—
infinite mothers are passé.

I give up GIVING
and will try the new flavor
TAKING—
but I may be allergic.

Muse of Merriment

set the table
lavishly, nothing spared
it's chocolate for breakfast—
why, today it's yes, yes, yes!
just blessing and bounty
no borders, no boundaries
why, today is the day
the remedy we seek
is yes, yes, yes!

Scherzo con moto

Chocolate for Breakfast

a perfect square of brown
edges sharp as raven's talons
melts to liquid painfully slow
as the tongue tangoes around
the taste buds awaken delighted
by this dawn's irreverent surprise
of chocolate for breakfast

sinful almost shameful
as the oatmeal stares in shock
from the cluttered pantry shelf—
there's no going back now

a second piece is disrobed of its foil cloak
and shoved down in a rush akin to
the seven a.m. train line downtown

my beloved milky mistress
can be counted on for her kicks and quirks
a touch of caramel
a kiss of sea salt
all the nuances that madden me more
and drive me farther from kale and wheat germ
than is advisable or safe
for regularity—

hell, if there were one day left to live
I ask of you this:

chard or chocolate?

Remedy

what ails you
in the corner
chin tilted south
you in the purple shade
nose in the book
binding self to word
much easier than facing faces

what ails you
blue-screen complexion
reflecting
others' lives
others' business
as you sit still
alone in the study
studying stillness

what ails you
lonely child
surrounded by self
and ghosts of possibilities
that you believe
not to be possible

a drop of this
I deposit
by your screen

a spoonful of this
I rest by your desk:

a wave of fresh spring grass
a hum of midnight cricket song
a clasp of friendship's warm hands
a silent partner
who trods along your side
knowing you are here
and glad of it

Dr. Death

Dr. Death
presided over the very
last
b r e a t h
whichpuffed like a stucktugboat
that
had no
more
t u g
Dr. Death
likes to stand
his back
up against the high wall
ice
cold
hands
clasped in a bony knot
knuckles popping
but
patient
oh so patient
for that last
that very last

g   a   s   p
he takes out the silver
shears
from his black silk purse
and snips
the string
that ties
bodiestohearts
in one calculated cut
he lets all the tapestry
U N R A V   E . . . L
and clumptothefloor
the portrait disassembled
permanently
oh, how Dr. Death
feeds on the snip
and moves from room to room
home to hospice
field to furnace
always alone
on the back high wall
knuckles popping

The Blessing

drips
drops
flows
floods
swimming surrounded by the enormity
no end to it
pure grace
no borders
total goodness
complete glory
truth and dominion
but sweet
like the ripest
peach of summer
but comforting
like the smoothest
worn pebble
but absolute
like the warmest
midnight dark
but compassionate
like the mother's full breast at dawn

Sing, Then

When there is mold growing
where there should be moss.
When there is doubt sown
where there should be promise.
When the giving comes from your blessed heart, alone—
sing, then.

When shadows fill the spaces made
from dreams you've since set free.
When silence rushes in through walls
cracked where you can't see.
When missing turns to habit—
sing, then.

Sing for tomorrow,
sing for the others,
sing for boats on distant waters,
sing for you can,
sing for you must,
sing for us,
sing, then.

Mr. March

Ahem …
I am Mr. March.
Pleeeease
open up.
Outer petals,
I'm knocking on your velvet hatch!
knock
knock
knock
Delicate ballet-pink curtains
seem so light—
nothings, weightless.
Yet how tight they band
together,
refusing my gaze, my grope,
and how I desire a peek
inside
the bud.
KNOCK KNOCK

Innocent bride
amidst the rampaging thistles,
you tried to hide
but could
not.
There, there.
Your dear tears
so silent, wet,
displeased
by your exposure
to shutters and oil paint.
Solitude does not become a rosebud,
my dear.
KNOCK KNOCK

NO
Solitude does
not
become a rosebud.

Shrimpo Giraffe

a short giraffe showed up for supper
he was feeling kinda low
we made small talk
for a bit
until we hit a hard
spot
and wrestled
neck in neck
munching on our words
like tasty hors d'oeuvres
getting thick leaves stuck
in our back teeth
we ambled around the backyard
until the sun tucked itself in
and then me and my shrimpo giraffe
got comfy on the corduroy couch
and read Shel Silverstein poems
laughing at bossy adults and annoying baby brothers
and that felt great

Glop

Glop is oozing
out from my pencil
my memory
my larynx

Glop is mama's
mud-brown offering
served on yet another school night
in yet another house
we'll soon abandon

Glop is holding
the segments of my
broken-mirror self
from crashing further down

Glop is the stuff
I promised to leave
but kept hidden in my shoe

Glop is the mistakes
I never admitted
but were printed on the front page of my
good morning paper

Glop is my juice
that should be
vitamin rich
but is so hard to clean off
with a normal sponge

Glop is the fuel
that drives my pen to work

Glop is the food
of fools who believe
that a diet of song
can fill the belly of a soul

Glop is keeping
me alive if only to record
how full a heart can be
against all odds

The Buddy System

Hold hands, buddies,
     clasp those plump fingers—
          intertwine
overhand, underhand,
     flip back and forth,
          as little ones do to get their sweaty palms
victoriously on top.
     Just don't let go.
          Hold hands
when sleek German shepherds bark,
     when the mercury drops below zero,
          when we fear we're lost but
no one's admitting it yet.
     Hold hands in prayer,
          hold hands to warm each other,
hold hands to convince ourselves
     there's something to hold.

Hold hands to balance
the you and the I
so we're both in step
as we march forward
into tomorrow's kingdom
where partners are royalty,
where holding half the riches
makes you the richest.

Bloody Bat Mitzvah

You lovely swarm—
on this auspicious day,
you become
mature bloodsuckers.
Today
you will spread your wings
and take flight
as your foremothers did before you
and your daughters will do
sooner than you can imagine.
You young thirsty spirits—
how sharp are your stingers,
how long are your needles.

A gnat of valor—
who can swat her?
You follow a long, illustrious line,
a glorious tradition
of silent, swift, segmented
mosquitos.

You are no longer larvae,
little levitating ladies—
you will soar and
you will conquer
if you hold these three golden rules dear:

One
Go for the butt.
There's no substitute for high quality juice.
Attitude is altitude, my loves, so set your sights high.

Two
Darkness is your friend.
Transparency seems ethical, but the righteous don't prosper.

Three
Suck and sail.
Loitering at the scene of the crime only invites a response.
So less is more, gals.

And so, as you take flight on this blessed day,
we say to you,
on behalf of the Synagogue Sisterhood:
Fly high, sting deep, and bring us all
true Yiddishe nachas.

Mazal Tov.

Yelp Yes

Autumn showed up on my front porch
with a sprinkle of honey leaves
and a blast of refrigerated air
thrust forcibly down my throat,
no apologetics offered.

The stale breath which had lazed in my lungs since July
made haste.
The familiar burning Mediterranean sun took her leave,
evacuating with a suddenness
that hatched
a prized space for
looming storm clouds and
dawn's heavy mist.
Now
the underlings must shift to find rays of warmth.
The crawlers and slithering ones pivot and jerk
in a confused waltz.
Feet are hesitant and voices call out from the forest
in question, in resignation.
Yet there are those unafraid ones
who yelp,
YES!

So Sorry, Daddy Long Legs

So sorry, Daddy Long Legs,
you spindly ballerina,
you will never be painted by Degas.
You were born into the wrong species, dear.
Your mama will never buy that sequined tutu at full price
and the pale-faced Madame LaCross will never berate your
    sloppy pliés.

Oh, I am so sorry, Daddy Long Legs.
Spindly ballerina,
you will walk the pebbled lanes
trying to avoid assassination by five-year-old shriekers,
and the glitzy stage at the Met will remain
as elusive as a firefly's convention in Jerusalem.
A pink-toed dancer born into a class of creepers
is DAMNED.
Destined to be flattened on a suburban sidewalk
instead of celebrated under the blazing white lights
of a stuffed Manhattan theater,
no matter how fine your legs.
But, OH, how fine they are.

Portraits that Convince

Peering close to my face this morning at six a.m.,
still black-skied outside,
staring at me
under the white lights in the clouded bathroom mirror,
surrounded by toothpaste splatter:
I meet my fifty-year-old portrait.
"Good morning, wench—
you look like you feel."
The crusties are still wedged in the corners of my eyes,
unwilling to get dressed
in black charcoal so early.
Twisting open Mac #83 concealer,
I slather my sallow skin with a youthful promise
I don't rightfully own.
"There, that's better.
Now you can convince the world you are absolutely worth
listening to."
The eyes in the mirror wink back.
"But, are *you* convinced?"

Muse of Majesty

what we know
amplifies what we don't know
whether it's holy
or whole
the sweet unknown
or bitter as endive truth
all of us loony dancers
in this grand marble hall
a sacred space
to make sense of the unknown
so we spin, flip, and dizzy ourselves
to the point of epiphany
all of us bobbing our emptyfull heads
arriving finally
at the same answer

Rondo espressivo

Mama's Boy

He puts on his smile
at sunrise Sunday morning,
along with his crinkled khaki uniform.
Taking neither off all week,
he wears that grin
the way you'd wear
a bulletproof vest
caught
in a Harlem gang war.

How can
a smile
protect and project,
repel and propel?
How do
twenty-two-year-old boys
wear love as armor?
Courage is a choice
he makes
for you.

My Man

He knows me
in my
lesserness.
He knows me
and waits for me to speak,
then listens with both eyes
and two hearts,
because I need more than one.
He knows me
in my nakedness,
in my ecstasy,
in my doubt,
in my pain,
and holds it all
in devotion and service
to love—
he knows me.

One Dance

I want one dance
in the middle of the marbled hall-
mark card that promises glittery celebrations
that plasters full smiles on barbie dolls
whose legs split perfectly but fall off
two is better than one except for
cockpits that hold solo pilots who
pee in their flight suits
first time up and over and out
WHAM
hit the sonic boom and deaf now
partially blind
to the truth
I only wanted to dance with you

it was too much to ask
not what your country can do for you
but why is there no real vowel in
why
if it keeps ringing as an anthem the world over
a national cry that
can't be cured like the common cold
as bitter as Saskatchewan cold in mid-Febrrrruary
as bitter as endive in the garden salad I ordered
without the endive
the end dive
I only wanted to dance with you

Creative Papa

You unwrap your dainty eighteenth-century violin
from its ruby velvet dressing,
planting it like a guillotine-in-waiting
on your thick hairy neck.
Your eyes find mine,
and surely nodding once,
direct me, as the plunker
of the opening chord.
It will be an A-minor triad
in the low register—
basic, so we can both improvise easily.
Minor chords are our steady diet.
Like kasha varnishkes with cheap whiskey,
they came over on that bloated boat
to stay.

One time through the melody,
straight, with no surprises.
But after that deception,
nothing will be ordinary.

You will toy with the timing,
rushing the downbeat
like a flushed tango dancer.
Unleashing runs in fury,
scattering harmonics in a crazed, driven hailstorm
that is both blinding and glorious
in its perfect chaos
as listeners are left
wide-mouthed and head-scratching,
unable to swallow the rush of fluid sound.

Wisps of corpulent Italian arias
shamelessly pitted against
the simple peasant's song
as time folds in on itself
and the earthen crust shudders
in utter displacement.
The sacred and profane are locked
in a deadly showdown
where neither can win, nor release the other.

Your stubby fingers press deeper into the fingerboard
as your bowing arm
drives the music harder still—
a relentless horseman, fixed on the setting sun.

There is no oxygen left between the measures.
The rests have long ago packed their bags.
My humble piano line has barely rolled out
as the fiddler's countermelody boasts
a perfect, terrifying crash landing.

I can't keep up, Pops.
But you're still driving the scales harder.

I can't keep up, Pops.
But you've changed keys. Again.

And morphed genres.
Rocking, waltzing,
then hammering.
Pelting me with more sharps
than I can calculate,
upping the tempo
full throttle.
Ten fingers, sweaty and thin,
struggling to grasp
some firm common ground.
My hands are left
crossed, swollen,
still
on the slippery ivories.

Sweet Pea in the Bulrushes

"You, sweet pea in the bulrushes.
Don't ya cry, don't ya cry," she hushes.

You will grow.
You will thrive.
You will keep your kin alive.

"You, sweet pea in the bulrushes.
Don't ya cry, don't ya cry," she hushes.

You will fight.
You will free.
You will dance across that sea.

"You, sweet pea in the bulrushes.
Don't ya cry, don't ya cry," she hushes.

You will run.
You will hide.
You will feel God by your side.

"You, sweet pea in the bulrushes.
Don't ya cry, don't ya cry," she hushes.

You will stumble.
You will stutter.
You will sing like no other.

"You, sweet pea in the bulrushes.
Don't ya cry, don't ya cry," she hushes.

I Will Not Know

If he loved her really,
if he really ever loved her—
why he hoarded infinite amounts
of Hostess double chocolate cupcakes under his broad bed
living in his red-roofed mansion;
why he stubbornly climbed down, then up, the Grand
    Canyon in one day after his diagnosis;
why he insisted on mending his own leather jacket with
    jagged stitches, like handiwork he performed on faces;
why he exercised in the nude, no matter how cold the winter;
why he didn't hesitate to buy that expensive Italian violin
    when his scales were that elementary, but would drive for
    miles to find cheap bananas;
why he slept alone for years in the master bedroom while
    she slept down the long corridor in Stuart's bed;
why he crossed out every reference to a Creator in his home
    library but insisted on a last prayer with his last breath;
why he loved limericks, candied almonds, and German cars;
why he laughed in the living room and cried in the
    bathroom.
If he loved her really,
if he really ever loved her.

Gloria

Gloria wore a name
that tramped through the snowy mounds
of Bereza a century ago,
singing the lullaby of Baba Yaga
in topsy-turvy Russian rhyme.
Navigating fifty years
in a shiny wheelchair, driving it
like a spanking new Lexus.

Gloria and her bold yellow pencil, ever sharp;
her kitchen cutlery, sterile enough to slice flesh in the ICU;
Sunday's crossword puzzle, sprawled out on the walnut
    table,
boasting complete accuracy, top to bottom
and all across,
like the brilliant diagnoses she doled out for free
never having attended medical school,
outsmarting your trusted pediatrician again and again.

She knew of your mounting fears
and spread words of comfort like a soft woolen blanket,
    pink and fresh,
over your shivering tomorrow.
She knew of your loneliness,
calling every Sunday, sure as the church bell's chime.
She knew the destructive path of the brewing winter storm,
and those waterproof mittens arrived before
the skies, ashamed, dumped the burden
they could no longer carry.

She coaxed Schubert out of her black-and-white confidante,
played the greats like others mow their August lawn.
She wiped away tears before they sprang,
keeping extra soft tissues
tucked in the pocket
of her heart.

If Only

The umbilical chord----------------------
\/\/\/\/\/\/\/ shaky line between
parent ~~~~~~~~~~~~~~~~and~~~~~~~~~~~~~~~~~~child.

      Cords feed or choke.
      Chords sooth or torment.

I notice my hearing, eyesight
getting worse with age,
but not my hindsight
which grows, a thorn
extracted at great cost.

I raised a son
who was peace.

He was the first wave to hit up the smooth sand at dawn
and the last wave to roll out with the North Star's nod.
He had all the time in the world
to suck in the strands of harmonica song
and strum days full of patterned notes—

music that lifted,
music that healed all the shattered glass
on the seafloor.

Clock, calendar, deadline:
suggestion, at best—noose, at worst.

> You know,
> sometimes adding punctuation to free verse
> or a stopwatch to lovemaking
> just
> kills
> it.

If only
I could have retired
as parent
and flopped beside him on the sand,
throwing my watch into the foamy waters,
singing harmony his way.
If only.
~~~~~~~~~\/\/\/\/\/\/\$$\/\/\/\/\/\/\~~~~~~~~~~~~~

Sweet Unknown

Adam KNEW Eve.
He took her. He knew her.
But what did Eve know and
what did she come to know?
The hard way, the long way—
the fruit that led to the
longest swallow in history.

One bite, they knew too much.
One lie, an eternity of unknowing—
crunch
chew
denial
nudity—
a swooshofdominoesfalling,
altering the scaffolding
of every construct since.

One bite, they asked too much.
One deception, a lifetime of sweat.

Did they know—
do we know—
if it was worth it?

Well, how sweet
was the fruit?

Three Rays

The log cabin that
floated across the globe,
Old Noah at the helm,
had a small but
critical
hole
where the sun poured in.
Three rays, max, but healing splendor
rushed through those
moist roof slats,
three golden arrows
shot like love missiles
from the firmament,
imploring the
fidgeting family
within
to believe
that shorelines are possible,
even
in a
damning deluge.

Faith is scarce
on a cloudless day.
But that Old Noah,
captain of a ship
with no rudder,
sailing between two worlds,
belonging to neither,
drank in the sunshine and grit,
sometimes gulped it down.

Three sons,
shouldering the burden of beast
and the crushing weight
that sons do carry,
would steal a glance
upwards,
re-imagining the light
as rainbow.

Such is the magic
of a window.

Same Answer

I am a silver candelabra in the bottommost drawer,
liberated just once a year from confinement.

I am a slippery bottle of olive oil,
impossible to grasp without dropping on
the marble floor.

I am a guilty heap of glittery gifts, most unaffordable.

I am a chipped white china plate, laden with greasy delights.

I am a people who light alone,
together,
worldwide,
each one praying
perhaps
to a different God, but all hoping for that very
same
answer.

Hole or Whole

Kadosh Kadosh Kadosh
High and Holy and Whole
(but bagels have holes
to make the bite worth it)

Kadosh Kadosh Kadosh
High and Holy and Whole
(but prisms have edges
to let the colors shoot forth)

Kadosh Kadosh Kadosh
High and Holy and Whole
(but the staff is full of rests
which shove the music off the page)

Kadosh Kadosh Kadosh
High and Holy and Whole
(but the face is full of holes
to let us sweat the heat)

Kadosh Kadosh Kadosh
High and Holy and Whole
(but black Hebrew in white space
allows for meaning)

Kadosh Kadosh Kadosh
High and Holy and Whole
(but wheat kernels must be crushed
to release their nutrients)

Kadosh Kadosh Kadosh
High and Holy and Whole
(but love must be lost
for ballads to sing)

Kadosh Kadosh Kadosh
High and Holy and Whole
(but holy are the angels
and whole are the men)

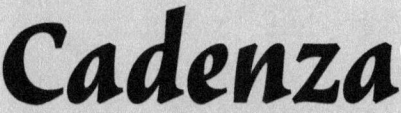

Birth Day

I gave birth today.
But my belly was steel, and my arms, wings.
I flew above the sands, precariously positioned myself, and
ejected a life.

Gracefully, he dropped.
      Gravity, the midwife.

From afar, one might view the scene with a romantic air.
The endless blue, the swaying body suspended by a drifting
parachute. The gradual descent tempered by soft winds and
a hazy skyline.

My son was never one for thrilling rides. Visits to the
amusement parks were more exercises in observation than
participation. Even as an infant, he made clear with his
piercing cries that being tossed upwards was not a preferred
sport. And as he grew into his teens, it was a hefty sci-fi
novel that turned a vacation day into a real treat, not a joy-
ride on a bungee tether.

Yet today was a birth day.

A treasure from above, he joined us finally on firm ground. Wet with sweat, naked of all possession. And those eyes— that told us of something big, known from beyond. We could barely sense the largeness of it, and the miracle hung there in the morning breeze, to be felt and let go. Miracles are like fireflies—they ignite our attention, but defy our grasp.

The past twenty years could not have been charted by the wisest cartographer. The trajectory lines were all drawn in pencil, an endless display of the journey's unpredictability.

We intimately knew of our son's gifts, and we equally feared for his flaws. His craft was built of strong stuff, but we were overly aware of the joints and seamlines; and I am ashamed to admit how we worried they would ground him.

Alas, son.
You taught us a grave and sobering lesson—that map reading the human spirit is like x-raying a rainbow.

I gave birth today, again.
Twenty years later.
From the swollen womb of a noisy, diesel-filled jet plane, dropped a hero in Israel. He landed, two feet on the ground, smiling, and looking forward.

Acknowledgments

Midlife plays with one's sense of timing. Gravity can slow us down, but mortality urges us to live more fully, faster. Two tempos at work simultaneously. And to complicate matters, often there are multiple lines playing at once. Reality is polyphonic. Sometimes that is glorious, sometimes unbearable. It is always interesting.

I rejoice in the wild and wide range of artistic influences in my life.

In the beginning, there were Mom and Pops and the five Epstein kids. Our home was a whirlwind of weird and sometimes wondrous experience, from Indiana to Hong Kong. Yet it was the powerful thread of music that tied the wonky tapestry together. Musical study, performance, and expression held an almost exalted religious status. As for our people, music ensured our survival.

I remember with abundant love my dear Aunt Gloria Benis, who, because of forces larger than herself, never got to enjoy her full scholarship at Oberlin and become the world-famous pianist she deserved to be. But she will always be a star in my heart because of her brilliant mind and loving spirit. Cleveland had her angels, and Rochel and Nate (obm) Berman redefined "the good life." We love you.

The years I spent studying jazz and classical music in Columbia University were joyous, and we sure appreciated those student tickets to Carnegie Hall.

My thanks to my gifted musical mentors: Kim Bova, Susan Krausz, Gabi Talroze, Oded Shimoni, Moriel Hoffman, and Gal Nyska—all artists who stretched my mental canvas as a musician, composer, and teacher of music. Learning how to hear sensitizes our spirit. And deeply understanding the scaffolding of music allows us to build a language that is fresh, profound, and hopefully coherent. There are many parallels between music-making and wordcraft; and I pray that, in this work, the reader enjoys the groove pulsating through the prose. If these words move you, quite literally, then I am gratified.

Joyce Klein taught me to endure the sting of critique that grows a better writer, and earning her praise was sweet. I pray that one day my original musicals, which benefited from her guidance, will spring to life again on the stage.

My editors Elli Sacks and Adina Kopinsky were so gracious with their precious time. Elli, an extraordinary mensch, composer, and writer, asked me the hard questions. Adina, herself a profound poet, shared her serious scholarship. I am grateful for their ingenuity and kindness. The patient and positive Lindsay Lusby took a modest manuscript and birthed a book—cover to coda! Brava!

My spirit has been fed for nearly forty years by the iconoclastic thinker, my dear friend, Rabbi Dr. Aharon Hershel Fried. He imparted the essential lesson of how to be half-sure and wholehearted. Mignone Rosenfeld, my weekly study partner of two decades, opened my heart and mind to the world of big ideas, but through her daily small actions, enlightened me more. Carol and Mike Dean taught our family about faith, hospitality, lifelong growth, and the transformative power of love. Our entire family is forever grateful.

And what is a spirit without a strong body to house it? My devoted running partner Adina Milstone, Barre guru Tanya Marciano, and the yogi Esther Elfassi all know what it takes to build an empowered woman.

To all my many students, past and present, who toil in the vast fields of sound and silence, I thank you for your bold questions, your irreverent dismissal of tradition, your glow upon mastery, and your lasting friendship. To Sylvia LaVine—by taking on Chopin at age 88, you've taught us all that artistic growth has no expiration date.

A special thank-you to my treasured friends who encouraged me as I poetry-bombed them incessantly. Efrat and Elli Schorr, Aliza Israel, Yael Unterman, Ruthie Amaru, Jonathan and Shulie Mishkin, Leora Davids, Keren and Asael Abelman, Ben Heligman and Ruthie Arkush, Wendy Goulston, Alona Cole, the Pinczowers, Dr. Tovah Lichtenstein, the Bergers, the Zuta sistas, Devorah Katz, the Kutliroffs, Debows, CB and Jeff Neugroschl, Gila Weinberg, Barbara

Balk, Shelly Eichen, Yehuda Goldstein, Sara Geveret Kfir, the Millman-Levine family, Heckerville, Alan Friedman, the Sandwich Sisterhood, Lainie Klein, Yael Levy, the poetry workshop members, and Sarina Furer who got me started. A special shout-out to my caring siblings: Avi & Michelle, Sara & Rael, Chaya & Josh, Yaffa & Shimmy.

What a blessing to live in the Holy Land, to walk her valleys and breathe her fragrant, figgish air. I thank God for this great gift (and my beloved husband, Michael Hattin, for having the dogged determination to move us here and keep us here).

I do not take for granted the gift of true love nor the immense obligation that accompanies it. Thank you, my precious Michael. We've cherished every moment together.

This collection contains a humble poem for each of our children. My heartfelt tribute to them is nestled between the non-rhyming words—a meager attempt to capture their complexity and glory. Elchanan, Shvut, Eden David, Emmanuelle Carmi, Akiva, Hillel, Leeba, and Miriam—to behold the metamorphosis is to meet the Divine. I love you.

About the Author

Rivka Epstein Hattin is the author of two poetry collections, *Movements* and *Winging It*. She has also composed two hit musicals, *Talking to the Wall* and *Esther and the Secrets in the King's Court*. A beloved music teacher, Rivka explores sound and rhythm with budding artists of all ages. Together with Michael Hattin, their five kids, and two grandkids, she lives in a bopping treehouse, where music and words are the steady diet. Before a full day of pianists wafting through the door, Rivka delights in long runs through the terraced hills, fierce coffees, and headstands on the roof.

www.ingramcontent.com/pod-product-compliance
Lightning Source LLC
Chambersburg PA
CBHW020755130626
46554CB00006B/2190